e Joy of the Seaso

reathed in

aditions from

steryear

Holidays

Edited and Compiled by Roger Howerton

home for the holidays

First printing: September 2001

For information write: New Leaf Press, Inc., P.O. Box 726, Green Forest, AR 72638.

ISBN: 0-89221-512-7
Library of Congress Number: 2001092043

Edited by Roger Howerton
Cover by Janell Robertson
Interior by Campana Design, Moss Beach, CA
Illustrations by Bryan Miller

Printed in the United States of America

Please visit our website for other great titles:
www.newleafpress.net

New Leaf Press

Christmas Wish.
Where the berries glisten,
Berries white and fine,
(None to spy or listen)
Kisses sweet be thine.

home for the holidays

*C*hristmas is that magical time of frosty noses and warm hearts, green Christmas trees and red Christmas stockings, Santa in the chimney and Christ in the manger. One song calls it the "most wonderful time of the year," and to many, it is that, with the excitement and surprise it brings to children's faces, the glittering and grand décor that come with it, and the friends and family for which we are so thankful.

The best part about Christmas is the joy of the season which can melt any Scrooge's heart. The stories contained in this book will hopefully evoke that "Christmassy" feeling of warmth and happiness that comes only once a year, when old acquaintances are renewed, and the heart becomes a bit more charitable, and home is where we all want to be.

The Christmas We Spent in the Barn

I remember it like it was yesterday. I was just a girl of eight or nine and it was Christmas Eve. Our tree was decorated beautifully and had several presents under it. I was so excited about Christmas – absolutely thrilled. I was an only child, and lived with Mother and Papa. We had no other relatives close enough to visit or spend Christmas with here in Wisconsin. Our nearest neighbor was half a mile away, so it was just the three of us for Christmas, and I just couldn't wait until Christmas morning.

I was standing beside Mother at the kitchen sink drying the dishes as she washed. I was looking out of the kitchen window as I dried, watching for Papa's lantern. It was pitch black outside, and even though the barn was quite a ways from the house, I could often see his lantern easily as he walked to the house from the barn. But I had not seen it yet tonight. Supper was over, and Papa had gone out in the pasture to see about a cow. "With this front moving in, she'll have that calf tonight as sure as the world," Papa had said. He had been gone an awfully long time. Of course, it seemed like a long time to me because we would have to wait until he got back for our Christmas to begin.

The sky had been dark and cloudy all day. The radio had forecast snow, and that made me all the more excited. There was still some snow on the ground, but it had melted some and was dirty now.

Papa put some wood in the stove and relit his lantern while he waited for us.

I was excited about having new snow for Christmas.

"Maxine, do you see him yet?" Mother asked.

"No, Mother, but he'll surely be along anytime now."

"I'm sure he'll be back soon." Mother smiled with that loving smile I'd always known. My mother was always kind and sweet, but here on the farm, she was also very tough when she had to be. Papa always said, "If you're going to be a farmer, you've got to be tough." Mother was just the right blend of sweet and tough. Mother was perfect.

The back door flew open and startled me. Papa came in, and some snowflakes swept in also. He had a light layer of snow on his hat and shoulders. "Dagmar, this cursed lantern went out on me again!" he said as he quickly closed the door. "It's already snowing and that wind will just about

knock you down! I got the ol' heifer in the barn,
but it took a long time; she kept trying to head off
to the timber. Her water's broke, and she's already
in a strain. Dagmar, you get the old blanket, and
you and Maxine come out to the barn with me. I
may need help from both of you."

"But, Papa, what about — "
I began.

"Now just you hold your
tongue, and get your boots
and coat," Mother said.
"And put a scarf over your
head." Mother had already
left the sink and was getting
her winter garments on.

Papa put some wood in
the stove and relit his lantern
while he waited for us. Then we all

went outside together. Instantly I pulled the garments around me tighter and Mother put her arm around me, pulling me close. The wind was freezing as it seemed to come in at every opening of my clothing. It was sharp and blowing fiercely and the frozen flakes felt hard and they stung as they hit my face. I could see the light from Papa's lantern was dim in the blowing snow, but I could see the ground was covered already. I'm so glad I felt Mother's protective arm around me. We didn't speak as we headed for the barn. With the howling wind, we could not have heard each other, anyway. We just needed to get to the barn quickly.

Papa had to let Mother hold the lantern while he tried to open the barn door. It was already frozen shut. It was never easy to open even in warm weather. When he finally got it to budge, it took all his strength to open it against the wind. Mother and I quickly went inside, as Papa let the door slam shut behind us.

It was still cold inside the barn, but the wind was stifled. Papa took the lantern and we followed him past the feed room and down the passageway where the milking stalls were to the last hay manger. As he held up the lantern, we saw the cow and she was a pitiful sight. She was lying there on some hay with her sides swelled, and mucus coming from her nose. Her eyes looked sad, and she let out a low moo as she looked at us.

Immediately, her body tensed as she strained with the labor. She put her neck straight out and, oh, the loud groan she made just broke my heart. She was breathing deeply, almost panting, and Papa had a grim look on his face. "Settle down, now. It's all right," he said gently as he patted her on the back. The muscle tension subsided, and her body sank back down to the hay as she relaxed.

"Oh, Dagmar. We really need that new vet to help us, but I wouldn't be able to get him on a night like this. I've had to help with other calves before, but this one doesn't look good at all." Papa already had a rope ready to tie around the calf's legs when they came through. He hung the lantern on a nail and the eerie glow it cast made things look kind of spooky. He bent down to see how much progress the calf had made, but the lantern just didn't give out enough light to see well from where it was hung on the wall. "Maxine,

would you hold the lantern for me?" I couldn't
reach the lantern, so Papa took it down for me.
As he knelt on the floor behind the cow, he said,
"Now, hold it close so I can see. Come around
to the side. That lantern won't shine through
my body."

Mother just stood silently, waiting for Papa to
give her instructions. Looking back, I think that's
why Mother and Papa got along so well. She never
told him what to do, or how to do it, unless he
asked for her advice on something. Mother was so
patient with Papa.

The cow's body tensed again as she strained.
As I held the lantern closely, I could see two
hooves coming out. "All right. Here we go," said
Papa as he got the rope ready. He put a slipknot at
one end of the rope and put it around the pair of
little hooves. As he cinched the rope, the cow

relaxed again, and the hooves and the rope disappeared inside.

The wind was still blowing fiercely, and the tin roof rattled near the corner. I could feel the sharp air coming through the slits between the boards in the outside wall of the barn. My feet were cold; my nose stung, and my hands were getting numb. I didn't have any gloves or mittens; Mother had put an old pair of socks over my hands, but I couldn't tell that they made any difference. I looked up at Mother, but I couldn't see her face for the shadow.

"All right, Dagmar," Papa said. When she strains again, you help me and we'll pull." Papa got ahold of the rope with both hands and Mother grabbed it also with both hands right behind his. I tried to give them as much light as possible as they steadied themselves.

It wasn't two minutes until the cow tensed

again. As she pushed, Mother and Papa pulled. Mother was pulling as hard as she could, and the loose hay under her feet slipped. She went right down to the floor on the hay. She let out a groan when she hit, but she never let go of the rope. The cow relaxed again, and Papa said, "Okay, okay." As I held the light closer, we could all see that progress had been made, as the hooves and little nose were now showing. The cow was still breathing heavily, and I couldn't see her face for the light, but I knew she would still have the mucus coming from her nose, and that look of pain in her eye.

"Here we go again," Papa said, and he and Mother pulled as the cow strained in labor once more. This time the head and neck came out, and when the cow had stopped straining, Papa quickly got the blanket Mother had brought and wiped the calf's head, drying it before the cold air got to it.

"Now, if we can get past the shoulders," he said, "we'll just about have it." The cow exerted all of her strength now; Papa and Mother pulled, and it was a contest, but soon the shoulders were free. They kept pulling, and the hips and hind legs came out with no problem.

"There, there," Papa said, and briskly wiped the calf down with the blanket. Mother watched intently as the newborn tried to lift its head. "Isn't she beautiful?" asked Papa. "A little heifer."

Mother was breathing heavily now and stepped out of the manger to sit on a milking stool in the passageway. Still holding the lantern, I moved with Papa as he carried the new calf around to the cow's face. She took in a very deep breath, smelled the calf, and then blew the air out right in the calf's face. "Let her rest for a few minutes," Papa said, "then we'll have to make her get up. She must get

Final Exam

A college student was taking a final exam just before the Christmas holiday. Having not studied, he became very frustrated with the test and finally wrote, "Only God knows the answers to these questions! Merry Christmas!" and turned his paper in.
When he received his graded test back, the professor had written, "God gets an 'A,' you get an 'F'! Happy New Year!"

up and move around some. C'mon Maxine."

I carried the lantern and stepped into the passageway as Papa found some milking rags on which to wipe his hands. "Thanks for the help, girls," he said, looking at Mother and me. "I couldn't have done it without you."

Mother said, "It is good that the calf is well, and the mother, too. We should thank God for His goodness to us."

I said, "Thank you, God!" I was really thanking

Him that this was over, and we could get
back to having Christmas. I could see
Papa smile at me in the dim light
from the lantern. Just then we
heard a sound with which we were
well acquainted by now. The cow
moaned and was straining again.

"What's this?" Papa asked,
getting back to the cow. "Maxine,
give me the lantern," he said as he quickly took it and examined the cow. "Dagmar, we
are twice blessed! Come help me again!"

Soon we were back at the other end of the cow,
but this time, the calf came right on out, with not
much help needed. Papa again wiped down the
calf, grinning. "This one's a heifer, too! Thank you,
God, for your bountiful blessings!" Papa put it
beside the first calf and the mother smelled of it

also. "We will make sure the mother can get up now," he said.

"I can get up. I can get up," Mother replied. Papa laughed and so did I. We soon got the mother to stand, and the newborns got their first meal. Papa gave the mother some grain, although she didn't seem too hungry. She kicked a little at one of the calves. "That's all right," Papa said to her, "You won't have them long, anyway." Papa was referring to the fact that we take the calves off of the mother so we can milk her. We feed the calves milk that has already been milked from the cows each day.

Soon, Papa was satisfied that everything was all right for the night, and we left some hay for the mother, and headed back down the dark passage-way. I was still cold, and had lost all track of time while in the barn. When we came to the barn door,

He then pushed on the door. It didn't budge.

Papa lifted the latchstring, but the outside latch
bar was frozen. He yanked a couple of times, and
we heard it come loose. He then pushed on the
door. It didn't budge. He took a step back, put
his shoulder down, and hit the door with all of
his might. It still didn't budge. "Let me see the
lantern," he said. He took the lantern and held it
closely to a crack between the boards in the door.
"Jim-i-ny!" he exclaimed. "The snow is already
piled against the door! There is no way I'll be able
to open it," he said. "Come on."

We followed him back down the passageway. I
could see the new mother cow's eyes shine silently

in the dark as she watched us pass. We went past the stalls and mangers and came to the door that leads to the holding pen. Papa tried to open it also, but couldn't. "Dagmar, this must be some blizzard!" Papa tried the other doors of the barn to no avail, but at last he found one in the lee of the barn that would open just enough for us to squeeze through. He opened it, and taking the lantern, put his body halfway out, his large frame snugly sliding through the narrow opening. He shone the lantern into the night and pulled his body back in after only a few seconds. "You won't believe it! You just won't believe it! I can't even see the apple tree just over the fence. I can't see anything out there except white and black!"

He just stared at Mother and me for a moment. We knew what he was thinking. We were trapped in the barn. We knew better than to try and leave.

We remembered Mr. Kyper and the blizzard two years ago. Well, I really didn't remember it that well since I was so young, but I'd heard the story enough that I might as well have been there. Mr. Kyper had been in his house as the blizzard was raging. He had wanted some potatoes from the cellar, but his wife protested his going out into the storm. He, being the stubborn man that he was, told her that the cellar was close enough to

The beginning of the modern department store Santa may have been as early as 1841, when a man was hired to dress as "Criscringle" by Philadelphia merchant, J. W. Parkinson, and climb the chimney outside of this store. Thousands of children stopped by to see him.

the house that he wouldn't have any problem. He went, but never returned. They found his body a few hundred feet on the opposite side of the house from the cellar, buried in the snow.

"Well, we'll have to make the most of it until the storm passes," Mother said. My heart sank as I thought of the presents waiting to be opened, and what if Santa passed us by because no one was home? I was already crying as we sat down on a couple of milking stools and the bottom step of the stairs leading to the loft. "Now, Maxine, honey, don't cry," Mother said as she put her arm around me. "Are you warm, dear? We'll use some feed sacks and snuggle down in the hayloft. That's all we can do for tonight. It's too dangerous to go out into the storm."

We sat there for some time, Mother with her arm around me, and Papa smiling at us. The lantern made strange shadows on us, and suddenly I forgot about being cold. All I could think about was that we would have no Christmas. No presents.

None of Mother's Christmas cake. No Santa Claus.
Nothing.

One of the newborn calves mooed. The mother
lowed softly. Papa said, "You know, it was in a
place very much like this, and maybe on a night
like this that Jesus was born." Papa began telling
the story — and no one could tell a story
like Papa could. As I watched his face
light up in the lantern light, and his
hands make motions to go with
the story, I began to feel warm
inside, and so ashamed that
all I had thought about
were presents and Santa.
Papa was wonderful.
Mother was wonder-
ful. I just felt so
loved at that time.
Then we settled in.

The wind howled, the tin rattled, the cows mooed, and Papa snored. We snuggled in the hay with all of our clothes and coats still on. I was really rather warm all night, except for my toes.

When I awoke the next morning, it was to Papa's soft calling to my mother and me. He had opened the loft door, and we went to look outside. Everything was white and most things were buried in the snow. Only the tops of the fences and the trees rose above the snow. What a beautiful Christmas day!

Papa used a lid from a barrel to throw down onto the snow that had drifted against the barn below the loft door. It was such a high drift that he didn't have far to jump when he jumped onto the lid. It kept him from sinking deeply into the snow. Mother and I had to use scoop shovels from the

The Christmas tree was still there (somehow I had imagined that it would be gone.)

feed room, but they kept us from sinking. It took most of the morning using the lid and the shovels, but we did make it to the house. Papa had to use a shovel to get the snow away from the back door, and we went inside our little farmhouse. The fire had gone out, and it was cold. We were all hungry.

The Christmas tree was still there (somehow I had imagined that it would be gone), and I glanced at the packages underneath. I thought I saw something different, and took a second look — a long look. My heart jumped. Yes, yes there were some new packages under the tree. I quickly raced to pick one up and read the tag. "To Maxine, From Santa."

"Mother! Papa! He did come! He did come!" I squealed with delight. We opened our presents, ate our Christmas meal, and enjoyed Mother's Christmas cake. It was a wonderful Christmas.

To this very day, I'm not exactly sure how those presents got under that tree. Many Christmases have come and gone. Presents have come and gone. Even Mother and Papa are gone now, but I'll never forget that time we spent Christmas Eve in the barn, and found those presents under the tree.

*The National
Christmas Tree
Association has given
a Christmas tree to every
president and his family
since Lyndon Johnson.*

when was Christ born?

*M*ost Christians celebrate the birth of Christ on the twenty-fifth of December each year, but historians are sure that this date is not correct. The biggest clue is the fact presented by the gospel of Luke that "there were in the same country shepherds abiding in the field, keeping watch over their flock by night" (Luke 2:8). Shepherds would not have had their flocks in the fields at night in the wintertime. The flocks would have been in a fold and the shepherds asleep at the entrance. It is only in the hot days of the late summer and early fall that the shepherds rest in the day and let the flocks graze at night. The truth is that no one knows the date of Christ's birth or the exact year for that matter.

*I*t's not important that we know the exact time of His birth, but what is important is that we know why He came and what that means for us. When Jesus visited with Zacchaeus, He told him that He had come "to seek and to save that which was lost." He wasn't referring to lost property, lost wealth, or lost animals. He was referring to lost souls. Every person is a lost soul until they accept Christ as their Savior.

Isaiah reminds us of our condition when he says, "All we like sheep have gone astray." Jesus said, "I am the good shepherd: the good shepherd giveth his life for the sheep." That's exactly what He did. Sin demanded a blood sacrifice for atonement. Christ was born and later gave His life as our sacrifice — He became the sacrifice for our sins — and is now offering the greatest Christmas gift of all to everyone. But just like any other gift, it is not a gift unless the receiver accepts it.

Be sure and accept this gift, and, in return, give Him your life. Serve Him with all of your heart, mind, and soul.

That First U.S.

Christmas

It was December 25, 1776, and destiny was in the making. We were at war for our freedom from the British. The cities were in the hands of the British . . . only the woods, the snow, and cold were ours.

On that night, the town of Trenton, New Jersey was ablaze with light. Houses were filled with German troops. Who cared about the ragged, tattered, starving, and dying roustabouts under George Washington's command? To these professional soldiers, Washington's soldiers were simply a "rabble-in-arms."

There hadn't been much to change these professional military minds. They had seen these Yankees run at Long Island when the Hessians

The abbreviation "Xmas" is not part of a concerted effort to remove "Christ" from "Christmas." In the Greek language, the symbol for the letter chi (the first letter of "Christ") looks very much like an English language "X." Thus, "X" is a very old symbol for "Christ."

"Silent Night"

holds the record for being the most-recorded song of all time.

had come out of the fog. General Sullivan and his men had been chased and caught, with bayonets driven into the backs of the Yanks. There was drinking and boasting about how they would catch that rebel, Washington, and take his head back to England!

On this Christmas Day, Colonel Rall lay at Trenton with three Hessian regiments, 50 Jagers, 20 British dragoons, and a detachment of artillery. At midnight, Rall gathered his officers about him and shouted, "Noch einmal! Glory to Gott and to the Foxhunter, freezing in the hills across the river!" It was a night of revelry.

But the despised Foxhunter was on the move. Drawing his coat tighter, Washington peered ahead into the darkness. He sat there thinking. It was the "fullness of time" for him, the enlistments of 2,400

Prohibition

42

In 1659, the Pilgrims passed a law forbidding the observance of Christmas with an imposed fine of five shillings. This law was not repealed until 1681. The law was stronger in Boston. Every man in Boston was required to work each Christmas day (unless it fell on a Sabbath day) and could be dismissed from his job if he failed to appear that day, and that law stood until 1856. Many employers required their employees to be at work at five o'clock on Christmas morning so they would not have time to attend any special activities before they came to work. Children who were absent from school on Christmas faced possible expulsion as late as 1870 in Boston.

The first stamp to commemorate Christmas was issued in Canada on Christmas day, 1898. The first United States commemorative Christmas stamp was not issued until 1962.

men still left to him were up on New Year's Day. It was now or never!

At 6:00 p.m. on December 25, his men assembled at the river and somehow they got horses, cannon, and men into the barges. Just after midnight, with nothing but chunks of frozen soup to gnaw on for rations, they pushed across the river. It was a good clean plan for dedicated men.

Suddenly Washington struck! He could have chosen no better moment! They wiped out the defeats of the past. Washington drove Rall and his 1,400 men out into the cold. It was the turn of the war – every post along the Delaware River had been cleared of the enemy! Christmas Day meant war, good against evil, just as it did on the very first Christmas Day!

—Robert Strand, *Moments for Christmas*

44

The Christmas Ship

In the late 1800s, wooden-hulled schooners and
barges were the backbone of the commercial trade
on the Great Lakes. Goods could be manufactured
in one city and easily shipped to other cities around
the perimeter of the lakes.

Every year before Christmas, beginning in the
month of November, several schooners would haul
Christmas trees from Wisconsin and Michigan's
Upper Peninsula to Chicago. They would sell the
trees to retailers who, in turn, sold them to their
customers. It was a very competitive business and
also very dangerous as the November gales of the
Great Lakes can occur suddenly and furiously,
wrecking many ships.

In 1896, Captain Hermann Schuenemann had
an idea to use his schooner to beat the competition.

He would pick up his load of Christmas trees, sail to Chicago, dock near a busy street on the Chicago River, and sell his trees directly to the customer. In bypassing the retail middleman, his trees could be sold at a much lower price, his volume would increase, and much profit would be made.

He loaded his ship down with Christmas trees and sailed up the Chicago River in the frosty late-autumn weather. Near the Clark Street Bridge, he put his marketing strategy to work with electric Christmas lights hanging from the mast and the sign "Christmas Tree Ship. My Prices are the Lowest," on the gangplank. Customers

would buy the trees right off the deck of the ship.

His idea was an astounding success. For the next sixteen years, he brought his wares to the same spot, and Chicagoans looked forward to the *Christmas Ship* every year. He gave many trees away to needy families and churches, garnering him the nickname "Captain Santa."

In late November 1912, Captain Schuenemann was badly in need of money to pay a debt, and knew he had to sell as many trees as he could. The weather did not look good, but he and his crew crammed the hold of his schooner with 5,000 trees and lashed another 500 to the deck and set sail for Chicago. Within an hour, the ship was caught in the worst of a Lake Michigan storm.

The ship battled the storm, but it was too much. Distress flags were sent up, and rescuers came from nearby Two Rivers, Wisconsin. As they approached, they could see that most of the sails were ripped or missing completely and the three-masted schooner was iced over. Suddenly, a snow squall hit, blinding the rescue team for a time. When the squall passed, the *Christmas Ship* and all its hands were gone forever to the bottom of the lake. A bottle was found with a scribbled note in it:

Everybody goodbye. I guess we are through. Leaking bad. Enwald and Steve fell overboard. God help us.

Christmas in Chicago that year was sad and somber for those who had learned to look forward to

In the United States, over 40 million living trees are erected each Christmas season.

the arrival of the *Christmas Ship* over the past
sixteen years.

The next year, a different *Christmas Ship* arrived
at the Clark Street Bridge. Captain Schuenemann's
widow, Barbara, and two daughters were there to
continue the tradition. The *Christmas Ship* was
back in business and would carry on for over
twenty more Christmas seasons.

Christmas Tree Origin

*The first resemblance of the modern Christmas tree was a fir tree
hanging with apples used in the medieval German play known as
the "Paradise" play. Around 1840, Prince Albert, the German
husband of the beloved Queen Victoria, set up a beautifully
decorated Christmas tree with an angel at the top in Windsor Castle.
The royal family was pictured around their Christmas tree in the*
Illustrated London News, *causing common folk to want a tree of
their own. The trend soon crossed the Atlantic to the United States
and Christmas trees became fashionable all over.*

The state songs of Maryland ("Maryland, My Maryland") and Michigan ("Michigan, My Michigan") are sung to the tune of "O Tannenbaum."

❧

With sales of over 30 million, Bing Crosby's 1942 recording of "White Christmas" is the biggest-selling Christmas record of all time. He recorded it in the not-so-Christmassy month of May as a tune in the movie "Holiday Inn."

Christmas Comes to Grinders Switch

Of course, most folks won't get off of I-40 to see the countryside, but if you're ever driving through the area, it's worth your time to drive down Highway 100 to Centerville to see one of the oddest tombstones of a hero that you'll ever see. At Centerville, you'll need to take the road toward Grinders Switch. There's not much of a town left now, but back in the days when the railroad was the main method of travel and shipping, Grinders Switch was once a contender for being the seat of Hickman County.

Well, anyway, the cemetery's about all that's left, but if you'll go through the old gate of the Mt. Zion cemetery and to the right, over on the end is the gravesite where – well, now, I'm getting ahead of myself. Let's go back a few years to a wintry Christmas Eve not long after the Great War was over.

It had already been a bad winter for December

Early Christmas Shopping

The prisoner approached the bench as the judge
asked, "With what have you been charged?"
"I was charged with doing my
Christmas shopping early," was the reply.
"There's no crime in that," replied the judge.
"Just how early were you doing
your Christmas shopping?"
"Before the store opened."

in these parts, and it was snowing again on
Christmas Eve. There was a layer of ice under the
snow and that didn't help matters any. Most folks
just stayed in by the fire and tended their livestock
when they needed to.

The Bradshaw children, Sarah, Cora, and Matt,
were just as excited this Christmas Eve as they had
been last year. They knew neither snow nor ice
could stop Santa from coming because he lived in
snow and ice year round. Their mother and father
were thinking quite the contrary, however. Uncle
Fess should have been here by now. He was to
bring the children's presents on the train from
Nashville. The Bradshaw's Christmas depended on

him. There was nothing
to do but wait.

Uncle Fess had left
Nashville on the 6:10,
bound for Grinders
Switch. He had meant
to catch the 1:30 ride,
but he had missed it,
and had to wait about
five more hours until this
one. The porter had just taken
his ticket, and he sat there with his
bundle of packages thinking about how
happy his nephew and nieces would be with their
Christmas gifts, and he thought he might as well
snooze just a little and enjoy the ride.

He dozed off, but was abruptly awakened as he
was thrown to the floor. The pack of presents hit

hard also, and the gifts went spinning and sliding
across the floor. Not many people were on the
train; one woman was screaming and a man was
helping her off of the floor. No one was hurt
badly, only a few bruises and headaches. Uncle
Fess hurriedly picked up the scattered gifts and put
them back in the pack as he listened to different
ones give their thoughts on what had probably
 happened. Soon, they all knew what had occurred
as the porter told them that ice and snow on the
tracks had caused the train to derail. They were
assured that someone was already on the way back
down the tracks to get some help. There was nothing
they could do tonight to get the train back on the
tracks, but they might be able to get a few wagons
to take the folks back to Primm Springs.

Well, that'll never do, Uncle Fess thought to
himself. With a word to no one, he promptly picked

up his bundle, got off of the train, and headed west toward Grinders Switch. He was immediately met with a driving, wet snow right in his face. It was very dark, and the tracks were covered with snow. Once his eyes adjusted a little to the darkness, he could pretty well make out the gap through the trees where the tracks lay. The best thing to do was just to follow the tracks. He wasn't sure how far away he was, but he'd get there sooner or later. He took long strides as he went, trying to walk as fast as he could. He had his head down as he went, and he thought of his brother's family waiting for Christmas to come. He wished there was some way he could contact them to let them know he was all right.

The snow kept coming and coming, heavy and already beginning to get deep. Although he had on a wide-brimmed hat and his overcoat, Uncle Fess felt wet and cold. The utter quiet pressed in around him as he walked on with that pack over his back. He stopped once or twice to "drink" some snow.

He had no idea how much time had passed. His feet were cold and hurting with numbness. He stopped and leaned against a tree to rest, setting his pack down. Suddenly a fear gripped him like none ever before. As he tried to peer into the darkness, he could tell that the consistent gap in the trees where the railroad lay was no longer there. He quickly kicked at the snow, trying to find some rails, but there were no rails. He looked back in the direction he had come, but he could not make out his tracks in the darkness and the falling snow. He would never be able to backtrack. He knew it would do no good to panic, and calmed himself, trying to come to his senses.

He tried to figure out if he were on a road, or near a field, but all he could make out is that he was still in the woods. He was so tired that he wanted to lie down and sleep, but he knew better than that. It was foolish to even think such a thought. He trudged on, but more slowly now.

The next morning, the Bradshaw family awoke to sixteen inches of snow, empty stockings by the fire, no Christmas and no Uncle Fess. The parents tried to explain to them that Uncle Fess had been coming with their presents, but they did not know what had happened to him. With the snow as deep as it was, there was no way to hitch up the wagon and go looking for him, and besides, they didn't know where to begin.

The only thing to do was to wait. Matt went with his father to feed the livestock, while the girls helped their mother with breakfast.

Three sad faces and two worried ones sat down to eat breakfast, but no one had much of an appetite. They just sat in a kind of a daze, not saying anything, but just picking at the sausage and eggs with their forks.

Saint Nicholas

*There really was a man named Nicholas who lived in
Asia Minor (what is Turkey today) in the fourth century.
His life is mostly legend built around scant facts of which
no historical documents remain. He was selected as bishop
of Myra, and as such he is often depicted with mitre and
bishop's robe of red and white, riding a white horse. His
good deeds have become legend. He became the patron
saint of Russia, Greece, Lucerne (and many other cities),
and, of course, he is the patron saint of children all over
the world. More churches worldwide are named for him
than for any apostle. He died December 6, 350, and this
date became St. Nicholas Day.*

Just then, the door burst open wide, and miraculously, Uncle Fess stepped inside. There were gasps and squeals and surprised looks as all five people got up quickly from the table and rushed to him. They had hugs and kisses for him, and he tried to smile, but was just too tired to make it into a grin, and he hurt through and through from the cold. They put him by the fire and then got him some dry clothes, hot food, and coffee. The children were delighted with the presents he had carried all the way. Uncle Fess felt good inside knowing he had made it home.

And that's the story of that Christmas at Grinders Switch. And, oh, yes, I almost forgot about that tombstone. If you'll go into the cemetery and to the right, over along the fence on the east side, look for a little white tombstone with this epitaph:

On this day we put to rest
The little toe of Uncle Fess;
Frostbite got it Christmas Eve
Nineteen hundred twenty-three.

The rest of Uncle Fess was interred many years later somewhere in California.

In December 1940, Mrs. A. E. Gadsby of Niagara Falls, Canada, mailed a Christmas parcel to her daughter in Prestwick, Scotland. The ship carrying the mails was torpedoed off the west coast of Ireland, but a favorable tide floated the package and unerringly cast it ashore on the beach of Prestwick. The contents were soaked but perfectly usable. The address was still legible and the package reached the addressee two days after Christmas.

— *Encyclopedia of 7700 Illustrations*

In December of 1891, Joseph McFee, a captain of the Salvation Army in San Francisco, offered a free Christmas dinner to the poor people of the city. It was a great idea, but how could he finance such a meal? Various ideas came to mind, but one idea stood out from the rest. He remembered that in his days as an English sailor, contributions had been collected for a worthy cause in a large pot placed by the docks, where plenty of people would pass by. After obtaining proper permission, he placed a pot at the Oakland ferry landing at the foot of Market Street and started a tradition that is now a familiar sight on many street corners and malls throughout the holiday season. From that start in 1891, the Salvation Army now helps over seven million Americans at Thanksgiving and Christmas, plus millions more in other countries.

Major Bill Hendricks founded the Marine Corps
Reserve Toys for Tots Program in Los Angeles,
California in 1947. Five thousand toys were collected
and given away to underprivileged children during
this first campaign. In the year 2000, over 15 million
toys were distributed in the United States and
Puerto Rico.

The first Christmas seals were printed and sold in
Denmark in 1904, originated by a Danish postmas-
ter who gave the proceeds to various charities. With
the Red Cross as the first sponsor, Christmas seals
were introduced in the United States, sold from a
table in the corridor of the Wilmington, Delaware
post office in 1907. In 1919, the American Lung
Association (then known as the National
Tuberculosis Association) became the
sole benefactor.

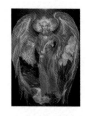

Courage

The Word "Christmas" comes from the Old English Cristes maesse *meaning "Christ's mass." In Middle English vernacular it was condensed to* Cristemas, *and finally to the modern* Christmas.

It was a few weeks before Christmas 1917. The beautiful snowy landscapes of Europe were blackened by war.

The trenches on one side held the Germans and on the other side the trenches were filled with Americans. It was World War I. The exchange of gunshots was intense. Separating them was a very narrow strip of no-man's-land. A young German soldier attempting to cross that no-man's-land had been shot and had become entangled in the barbed wire. He cried out in anguish, then in pain he continued to whimper.

Between the shells all the Americans in that sector could hear him scream. When one American soldier could stand it no longer, he crawled out of the American trenches and on his stomach crawled to that German soldier. When the Americans realized what he was doing they stopped firing, but the Germans continued. Then a German officer realized what the young American was doing and he ordered his men to cease firing. Now there was a weird silence across the no-man's-land. On his stomach, the American made his way to that German soldier and disentangled him. He then stood up with the German in his arms, walked straight to the German trenches and placed him in the waiting arms of his comrades. Having done so, he turned and started back to the American trenches.

Suddenly there was a hand on his shoulder that spun him around. There

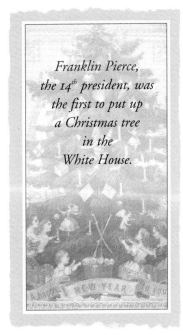

Franklin Pierce, the 14th president, was the first to put up a Christmas tree in the White House.

USES FOR FRUITCAKE

10.
Save it until next summer and use it as a boat anchor.

9.
Take it to the office and use it for a paper weight.

8.
Keep it at home and use it for a doorstop.

7.
Use it as a step stool in your kitchen.

6.
Let the little kids use it as a booster seat.

5.
Save it for summer and use it for a flower press.

4.
Carry it in your trunk to use in emergencies for a tire block.

3.
Put it in your workshop and use it for an anvil.

2.
Save it until next year and use it as a Yule log.

1.
Save it until next year and give it back
to the person who gave it to you.

stood a German officer who had won the Iron Cross, the highest German honor for bravery. He jerked it from his own uniform and placed it on the American, who walked back to the American trenches. When he was safely in the trenches, they resumed the insanity of war!

Courage takes many forms. It's a human trait that we all recognize when we see it in action.

The example of Mary and Joseph is perhaps history's most important moment of courage. In a hostile time (it was King Herod's territory, don't forget!), this young couple saw a pregnancy through and helped bring the King of kings into the world. What a marvelous display of courage and love for a world that is oftentimes lacking.

— Robert Strand, *Moments for Christmas*

A MERRY
CHRISTMAS
AND A HAPPY NEW YEAR.

In the year 2000, the United States Postal Service sorted and delivered over 20 billion cards, letters, and packages during the holiday season. Forty thousand temporary seasonal employees were added to

handle the workload as thousands of postal trucks, dozens of trains, over 80 supplemental airplanes, and over 60 million sacks and trays were also added to the already large network. December 18 was the busiest day of the season as more than 21 million customers mailed more than 300 million pieces of mail.

I'll Be Home For

Christmas

In 1939, my husband and I were young Christians who felt a call on our lives to go into the mission field. We left our home in Sedalia, Missouri and traveled by train to San Francisco, and then by boat through various stops in the Pacific, finally arriving at Jayapura, on the north coast of the island of New Guinea. Actually, my husband had gone there first, but, since the interior of New Guinea was a hostile area, I didn't arrive until a few months later, being the first white woman to cross the mountains into the interior.

It had been very dangerous for any white person to be among the native people there. The missionaries who had gone there before my husband were unsuccessful in their attempts to evangelize them. Those people had never seen the

other side of the mountains that boxed them in.
They called this unknown region on the other side
of the mountains the "spirit world," where the
spirits of dead people go. Since the white men had
come from the other side of the mountain, they
must be spirits, but it was strange to the natives
that these spirits had flesh. So, the natives had a
brutal test for these white men. The natives would

throw a spear at them. If the spear went through them with no harm done, they were spirits. If they bled and died, they were only men. Of course, the missionaries were only men, and many died before the tribe was convinced that the white men were friendly. Thankfully, this practice had been discontinued before my husband arrived.

Even after the natives became friendly, it did not cause the area to become a paradise. Situated only a few degrees south of the equator, it was exceedingly hot and extremely humid with torrential rains, swamps and mosquitoes. But it became home to me, and those natives became my family as we taught them about the love of God and the atonement of Jesus Christ.

Being totally committed to living among those people, learning their language, and adapting their ways while teaching them God's ways, we had no contact with the outside world. So we were taken totally by surprise when Japan invaded and took possession of the island early in 1942. (We had had no way of knowing about the conflicts in Europe, the attack on Pearl Harbor, or any world war until then.) The Japanese invaders left the natives alone, but took the missionaries and their families to two internment camps along the coast. The men were separated from the women and placed in a camp a few miles away; I wept as my husband was taken from me.

The Lord has blotted out of my memory a lot of the horrible events that happened at that internment camp, but some things I'll never forget. We were made to cook and do laundry for the Japanese soldiers. We kept gardens for them and built roads for them. I remember carrying heavy sacks of rice on my back as we unloaded trucks of supplies. I had no shoes and only one dress the whole time, but the dress miraculously lasted through all of the labor. At night, the heat was suffocating as we lay in beds under mosquito netting. More than once I had a huge rat get under that net with me.

Among other things, I was tortured by the Japanese as a guard thumped me between the eyes by flicking his index finger off of his thumb until my eyes turned black. I was accused of being a spy and kept in a prison cell, sentenced to die. While in that cell, I remember once being given a bowl of rice to eat that looked like it had cream on top, but the cream seemed to "squirm" and turned out to be maggots. There were so many times that I asked God, "Why have you forsaken me?" And He would answer me (not audibly, but in a still, small voice) so sweetly, "I will never leave thee nor forsake thee."

"I will never leave thee
nor forsake thee."

After several weeks in that prison, the Lord miraculously got me out and back to the prison camp. It was then that I found out that my husband had died while in the other camp. I went into a stupor. I moped for days. Knowing I would never see him again, I thought my world had ended. I questioned God, "God you've taken away everything from me, but did you have to take Henry?" He answered me again, "That the trial of your faith, being much more precious than of gold that perisheth, though it be tried with fire, might be found unto praise and honor and glory at the appearing of Jesus Christ."

Finally, the day came when some Australian

soldiers liberated those of us left alive in the camp. They told us the war was almost over and the Japanese were retreating from the island. We were glad to hear the news of the Allies winning the war, but we had no idea what month, day, or year it was. One day is just like the next when you're that close to the equator. I asked a young soldier boy, and he told me that it was August of 1945. It was amazing to think that so much time had passed, and then again, it had seemed an eternity.

We were given Red Cross packages, and then transported by boat to Sydney, Australia. There we were allowed to take the first showers we had had in years. (We took our time, too.) We were clothed, fed, and taken care of very well.

There was not much transportation available at that time to civilians because of all the soldiers going home. By the time I left Australia on board a

ship headed for the states, it was early December. I
was hoping I could get back to Mother and Dad in
Missouri by Christmas. I had not been able to
contact them since I had left home in 1939.

Even by December, there was very little room
on the ship because of the people trying to get
home from the war. I had no money, but I knew
that once I reached United States soil, I would
need money to go on home. Someone told me that
if I could find a Red Cross person, they would be
able to give me some money. Once again, the Lord
helped me find the very person who could help
me — right on that ship.

After days at sea, the ship was finally approach-
ing San Francisco, and everyone on board was so
excited . . . for a while. Then the ship started
moving away from the bay, and we were told that
there was no room for any more ships to unload in

San Francisco, and that we would have to go to Seattle. Many people were very upset, but I was not angry to have to spend a couple more days on board.

We finally docked, and I was so happy to arrive in Seattle, but I was still far, far away from Missouri. I asked directions, and had to walk several blocks, but I finally found a train station and went to the ticket window. "I would like a ticket for Sedalia, Missouri, please," I said.

"Whoa! Hold on there a minute, lady. Haven't you heard? There's been a war. Nobody is traveling except military personnel." My heart sank.

"But you don't understand," I pleaded. "You see, I've been gone from home for many years. I'm a missionary and I've been in a prisoner-of-war camp, and I must get home to my family." I began to cry.

He looked at me and smiled. "Well, I've got just the special ticket for someone like you."

He turned around and got some papers off a desk. He asked my name and some other information, and filled in some blanks on the papers. "Here you go," he said. "Just take these over to the airport and ask for a man named John Tillman in the post office there. He'll know what to do."

"Thank you very much, sir," I said. "Oh, by the way, what date is it?"

"It's December twenty-third. Merry Christmas," he replied.

"Thank you." And I was off. I don't know how the Lord kept doing it, but He was constantly blessing me.

At the airport, I was told that I could ride as an extra passenger in an airplane owned by the postal service to Kansas City. It was the first time in my

life that I had
flown, and I
was quite
scared at first,
but was soon
asleep in a small
space behind the pilot
surrounded by bags of mail
and packages.

Upon arrival in Kansas City, I found the nearest telephone, and called Mother and Dad. It was December 24, 9:42 a.m. I was so excited and wanted to hear a familiar voice so badly, but my heart was saddened once again when no one answered the telephone. I wondered where they could have gone on Christmas Eve, but Mother was always late with her Christmas shopping, so I put the worrying out of my mind.

Since the airplane flight to Kansas City had cost me nothing, I still had the money from the Red Cross. I quickly found a nearby bus terminal.

"How much to Sedalia, please?"

"Three dollars and ninety-five cents."

I had five dollars, and I was in business.

On the bus, I sat next to a woman who must have been about sixty. She liked to talk. Oh my, did she ever like to talk! "You just don't know what it's like. My whole life has been problems. My cat won't eat the cat food that I give her, and I can't afford any of those expensive brands that everyone else gives their cat. My neighbors like this big band music, and they play their radio so loud it gives me a headache. And my rheumatism is acting up again. These seats aren't very comfortable, are they?"

I smiled and said, "They're fine."

She looked back at me and said, "Now what do you do?"

"I'm just returning home from New Guinea," I said.

"Well, I've never been to Africa myself, but Mrs. Simpson next door has a son . . ." and she was off again, but I began to think about home and Mother and Dad.

Sedalia never looked so good to me as that bus pulled into town. Once I got off the bus, it was nothing to walk the five blocks home. The air was brisk, and they had already had a little snow, but the sidewalks were not icy. As I rounded the last corner, I stopped when I saw the house. My steamy breath was very visible in the cold air and I panted a little. My heart beat fast.

The old two-story house never looked better

with all of its windows and the porch that wrapped
in a U shape around the front room. There was a
gold star in the window (my brother had been in
the service), and lights along the top of the porch
railing. I began to cry as I saw a familiar Christmas
wreath on the front door.

I calmly walked across the street to 319 Cherry
and walked up the sidewalk to the front door. I
lifted my hand to knock, but hesitated just a bit as
butterflies rushed through my stomach. It had been
so long. I thought about just opening the
door and walking right in, but I felt
a bit uneasy about that since
Mother and Dad weren't
expecting me.

Finally, I took a deep breath
and knocked. I waited, and waited,
and knocked again. Then I heard a

The door opened and my
heart fluttered as I began to see...

thud, thud, thud, as someone was walking toward
the door. The door opened and my heart fluttered
as I began to see space between the door and the
jamb. I breathed deeply and smiled and looked
right at — someone I didn't know.

"Yes, can I help you?" the woman asked politely.

"Well, um, yes, I — " I was astonished. Who
was this woman, and where was my family? "Yes," I
finally said plainly, "I'm looking for the people
who used to live here, Mr. and Mrs. Bell. Um, I'm
their daughter."

"Oh, you must be Iva! Well, they still live here,
dear. Come on in! I'm their next-door neighbor,

Wanda Asbury. They're in the other room. I told
them just to sit still. I would get the door. They've
both had colds, and I brought over a pot of soup
for them. They've told me all about you. They will
be so glad to see you!"

By this time, we were in the front room, and I
heard my mother's voice for the first time in years.
"Who is it, Wanda?" My heart stood still. I was
overwhelmed with a gushing feeling of joy at the
sound of my mother's voice. Before I could reach
the kitchen door, she appeared in the doorway. She
just froze when she saw me. Her mouth dropped
open, and she put her hands over her mouth and
her eyes filled with tears. She stood there for what
seemed like a few minutes, just staring and crying.
Then she rushed to me and hugged me like she
would never let me go. "I thought I'd never see
you again. We've been praying and praying for

you. Why didn't you get ahold of us? Why didn't you write? Richard! Richard! Come here!"

Then Dad stepped into the room, and he was just as happy to see me as Mother was. All I could say was "Merry Christmas. I'm home."

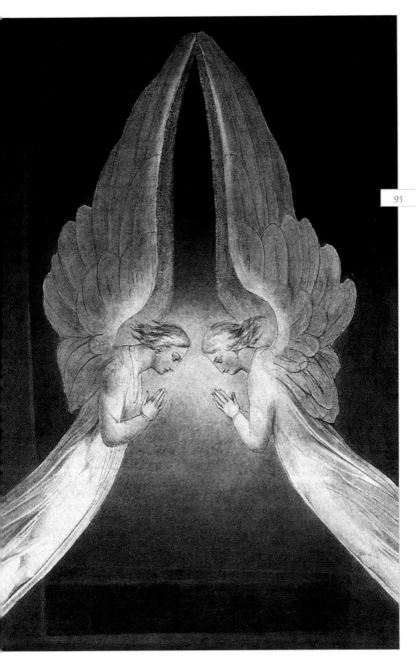

the end